Quotes Are Life...

Written and Illustrated by

Niki Kawa

Library of Congress Control Number: 2014913799

CreateSpace Independent Publishing Platform,

North Charleston SC

An Amazon Company.

CreateSpace and logo are registered trademarks of
Amazon.com, Inc.

Visit us on the Web!

www.nikisquotes.com

ISBN: 13:978-1500286750   ISBN-10: 1500286753

Niki Kawa supports the First Amendment and celebrates the right
to read.

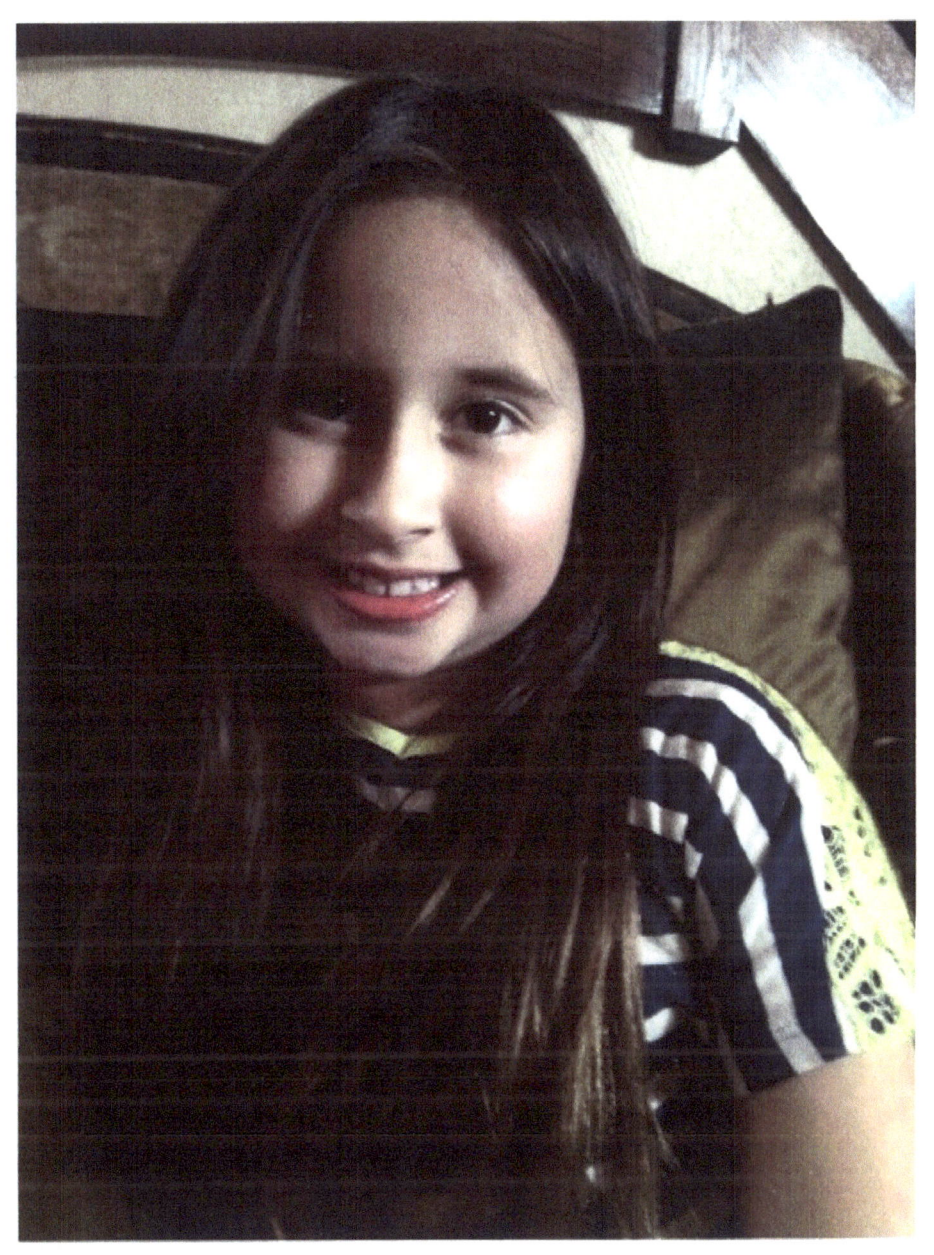

"To all of the people who have helped
me in life, this one is for you."
- Niki Kawa

To: Mrs. Alison Lubart, Mrs. Lauren Fisher, Mrs. Starr Lifson, Mrs. Brook Moody, Mrs. Kimberly Kent. To all of you thank you for your patience and knowledge!

Love, Niki Kawa

Tell me and I forget.
Teach me and I remember.
Involve me and I learn.

Benjamin Franklin

I cannot teach anybody anything.
I can only make them think.

Socrates

I dedicate this book to
my brother Mikey, my mom,
dad and my Grandparents.
I love all of you very much !

I want to give my love to
my Grandma Maria "Tata"
for her dedication to me.
(TE AMO TATA)

Love,
Niki

Education breeds Confidence.
Confidence breeds hope.
Hope breeds peace.

Confucius

I do not feel any
age yet.
There is no age for
spirit.

Unknown.

If you treat every situation as a life-and-death matter, you'll die a lot of times.

Van Wilder

Take your work seriously
but yourself lightly.

George Burns

In three words I can
Sum up everything I've
learned about life:
"It goes on"

Robert Frost

Every disappointment or challenge
is an opportunity for growth.

Niki Kawa

When you don't know what
to do... PRAY.

Niki Kawa

You earned it
Enjoy it!

Niki Kawa

Follow your dreams to get
to your wishes...
Follow your wishes to get to your
future...
Follow your future to get to you're life.
Niki Kawa

The more you like yourself,
the less you are like anyone
else, which makes you unique.

Walt Disney

Promise yourself to be so
strong that nothing can disturb
your peace of mind.

Christian D. Larson

Fall   seven   times   stand   up
        eight.

                    Japanese-proverb

You   never   fail   until   you   stop
trying

                    Albert   Einstein

A real friend is one
who walks in when the
rest of the world walks
out.

Walter Winchell

Forever is a long time,
but not as long as it was
yesterday.

Unknown

To handle yourself,
Use your head ;
to handle others use
your heart.

Eleanor Roosevelt

The best way to make your
dreams come true is to wake up.

Paul Valery

Be yourself:
Everyone else is already taken.

Oscar Wilde

To be a champion
believe you're the best.
If you're not, pretend you are.
        Mohammad Ali

Life is hard but it's your choice to make it easier.

Niki Kawa

I believe God created me.
He also gave me the
opportunity to learn and
get stronger, to create my
own destiny.

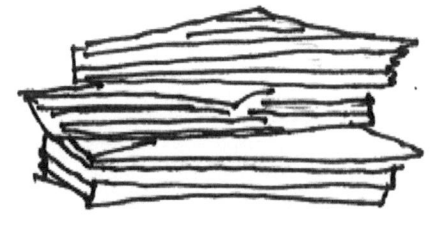

Harold S. Kushner

Good friends are like stars, you don't always see them but you know they're always there.

Unknown

A journey of a thousand miles starts with a single step.

Confucius

Show me your friends and
I will show you your future.

Unknown

When you say it's too hard you are close to doing something amazing.

Unknown

Problems, are opportunities
with thorns in them.

Unknown

You will never see a rainbow
looking down.

Charlie Chaplin.

Life isn't about waiting
for the storm to pass.
It's about learning to
dance in the rain.

Vivian Greene

The same fence
that shuts others out
shuts you in.

Bill Copeland

When you get to the end of
your rope tie a knot and hang on.

Theodore Roosevelt

A bad attitude is like a
flat tire, you can't go anywhere
until you change it!

Unknown

When love and skill work
together expect a master-piece.

John Ruskin

We don't know who we are
until we see what we can do.

Martha Grimes

Integrity has no rules.

Albert Camus.

Life is a ride and treasure
of surprises.

NIKI Kawa

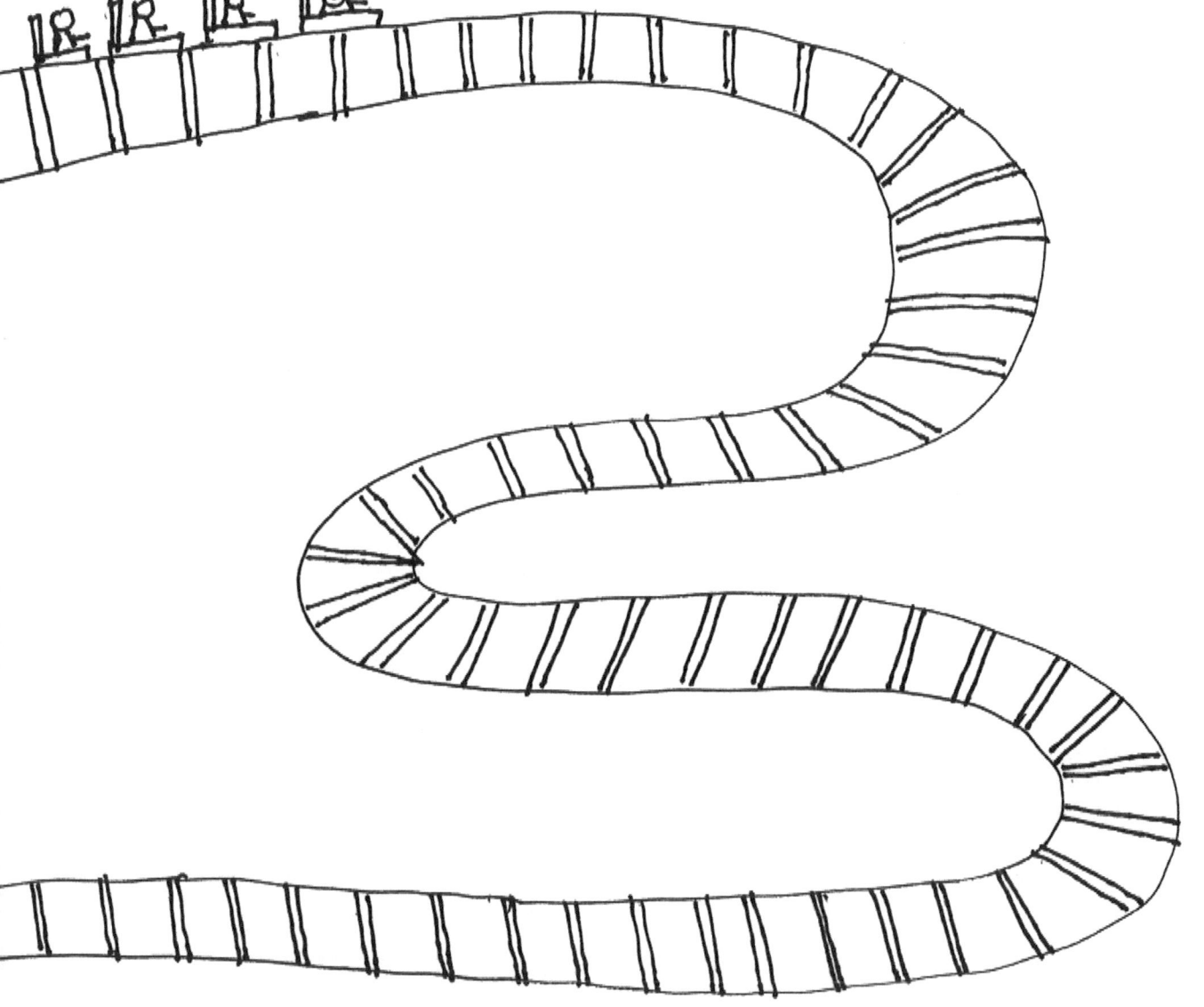

Don't be afraid to do the things
you love.

NiKi KaWa

Remember... People who try
to whittle you down are
only trying to reduce you
to their size.

Unknown

or...

Mean
Person

nice
Person

can be

Your thoughts are the architects
of your destiny.

David O. McKay

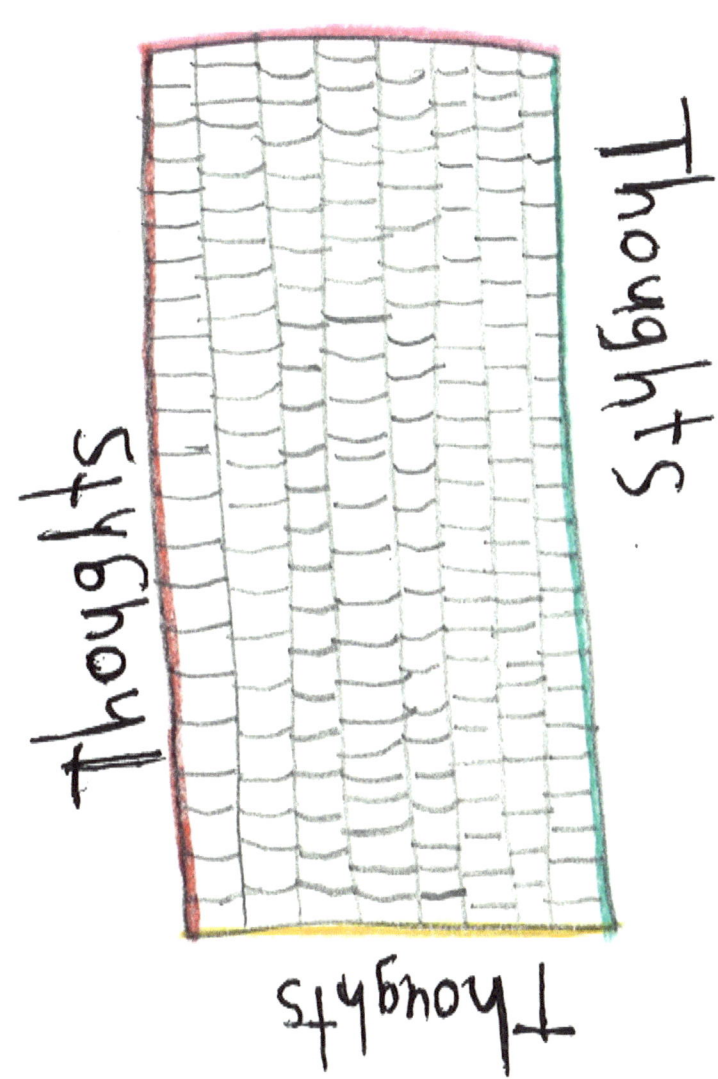

He who loses money loses most.
He who loses friends loses more.
He who loses faith loses all.

Eleanor Roosevelt

I know God won't give me anything
I can't handle. I just wish
He didn't trust me so much.

Mother Teresa

Sometimes I've believed as many
as six impossible things before breakfast.
Lewis Carroll

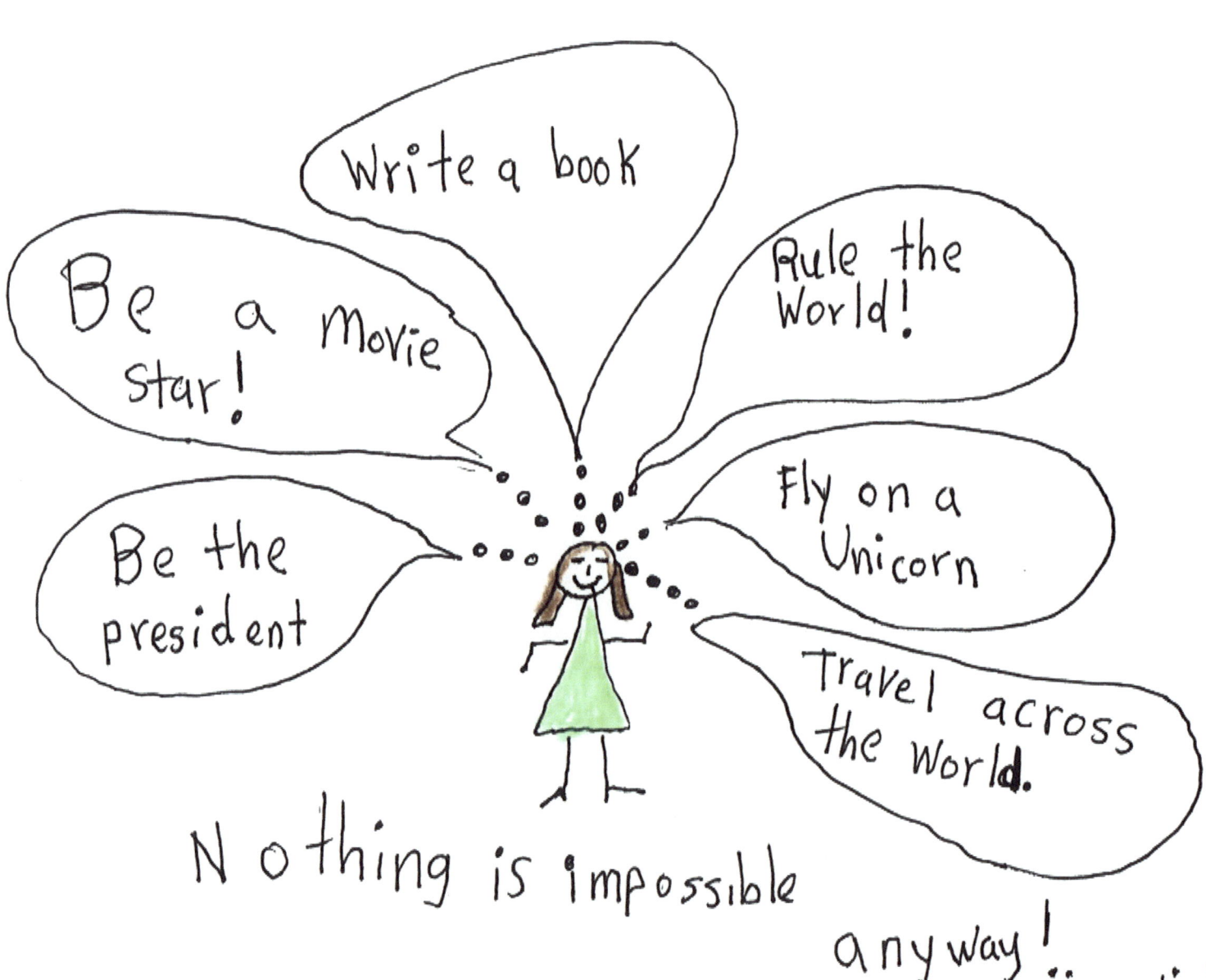

We have nothing to
fear but fear itself.

Franklin D. Roosevelt

We do not remember days,
We remember moments.

Cesare Pavese

The trick is growing up
without growing old.

Casey Stengel

Only in the darkness can you see
the stars.

Martin Luther King jr.

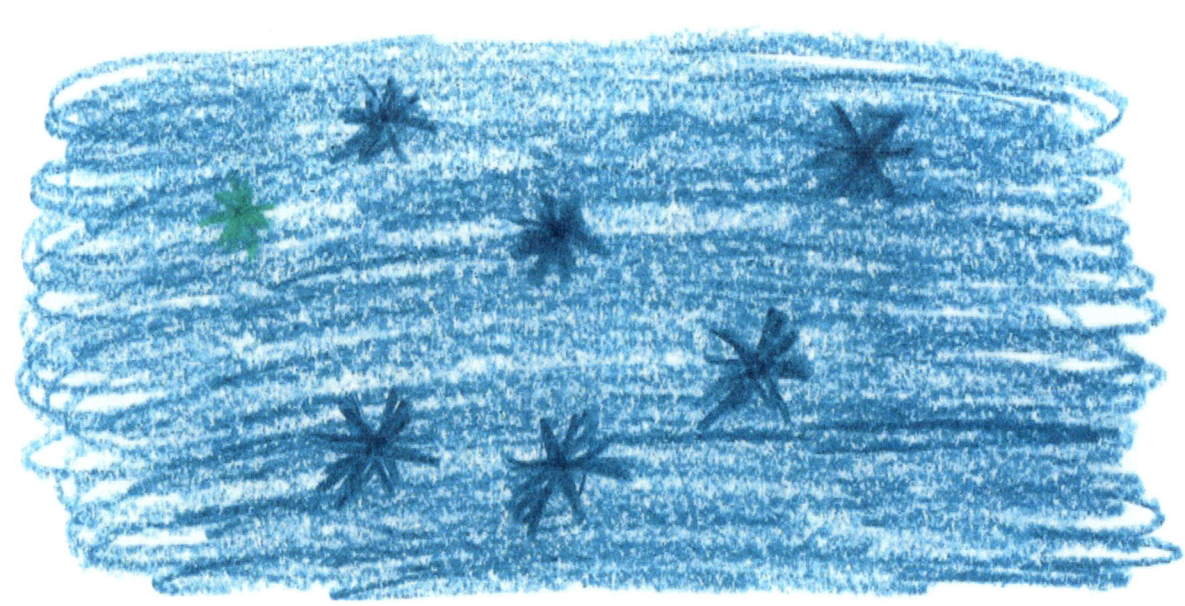

If you're going through hell
keep going.

Winston Churchill

Ask not what your country can do for you,
ask what you can do for your country.
John F. Kennedy (1917-1963)

Some people who have the
least have the most.

Niki Kawa

I love

to spend
time with
mom

A secret is what you tell someone else
not to tell because you can't keep it
to yourself.

Unknown

Success is the ability
to move from one failure
to the next failure with
enthusiasm.

Winston Churchill.

Remember God is ALWAYS with you;

Niki kawa

Gods Location